Capoeira: The Fighting Dance

Rob Waring, *Series Editor*

Australia • Brazil • Japan • Korea • Mexico • Singapore • Spain • United Kingdom • United States

Words to Know

This story is set in the South American country of Brazil. It happens in the state of Bahia [bəhiə], in the capital city of Salvador [sælvədɔr].

 Dance or Fight? Read the paragraph. Then complete the definitions with the correct form of the underlined words.

This story is about a Brazilian martial art called *capoeira* [kæpuɛərə]. This unusual art form is really a combination of both dancing and fighting. In the 1800s, slaves in Brazil invented *capoeira* as a way of fighting against their owners and it later became a popular activity. Like most martial arts, practicing *capoeira* brings together the body, mind, and soul. Also like martial arts, students of *capoeira* learn from a very experienced teacher, who is sometimes called a master.

1. A _____ is someone who is forced to work for no pay.
2. A _____ is a traditional skill of fighting that is done as a sport.
3. A _____ refers to a person who is very skilled in doing something.
4. A _____ is a mixture of two or more things.
5. The _____ is the part of a person that is not physical, which some people believe continues to exist after death.

B Street Kids.
Read the definitions. Then complete the paragraph with the correct form of the words.

at risk: in a situation where something bad is likely to happen
beg: ask for food or money on the street
crime: an illegal activity
homeless: having no place to live
social worker: a person whose job is to help people who have problems because they are poor, old, or have difficulties with their family

In many countries of the world there are street children and teens who are (1)_____ and must live without the care of parents or other adults. These kids often live in old, unused buildings, cars, parks, or on the street itself. Some have to (2)_____ for money with which to live. Others start committing (3)_____, such as stealing cars or money, to survive. Street kids are really (4)_____ for getting into difficult, dangerous situations. In this story, you will read about a group of (5)_____ who are trying to help the street kids of Salvador.

Practicing Capoeira

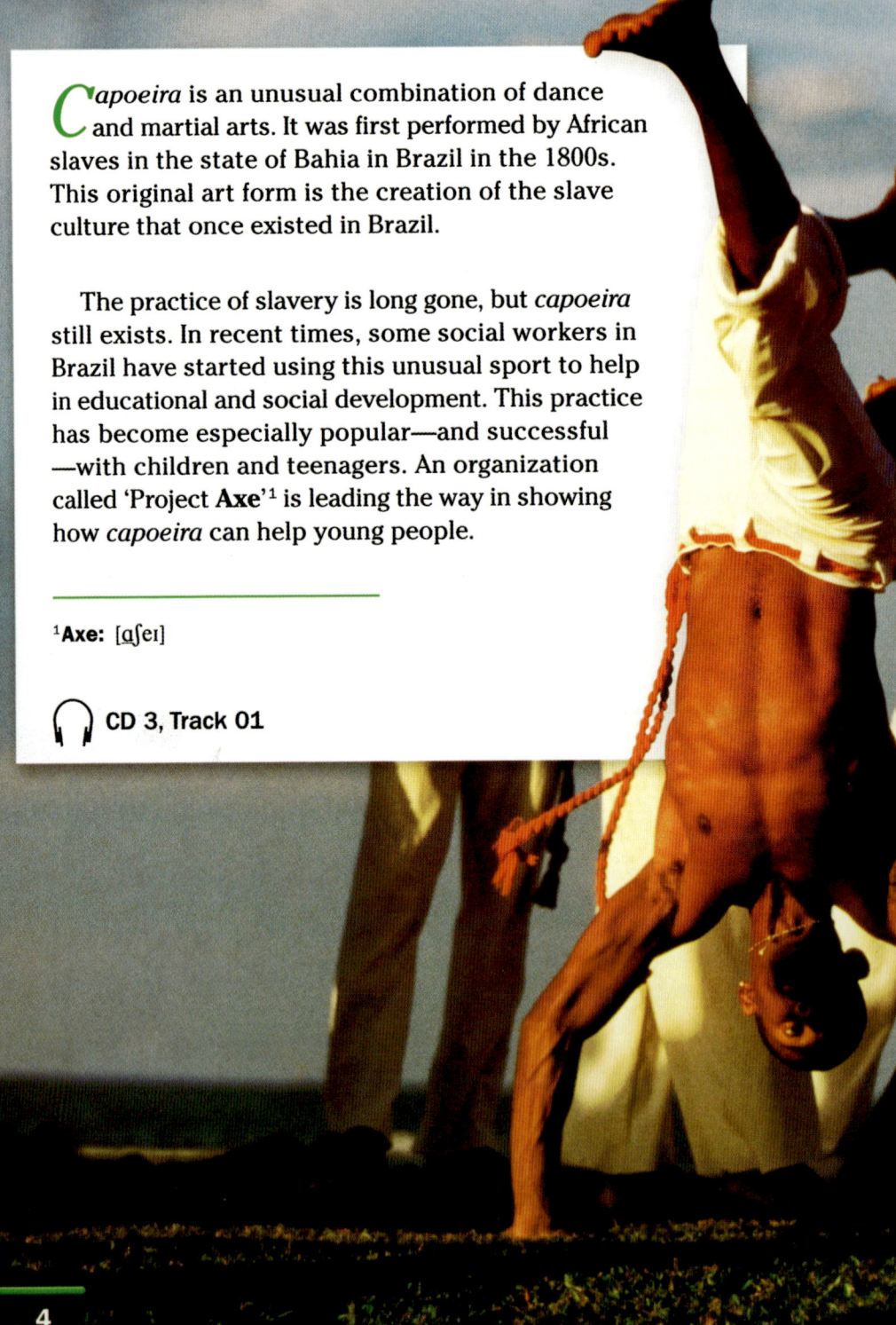

Capoeira is an unusual combination of dance and martial arts. It was first performed by African slaves in the state of Bahia in Brazil in the 1800s. This original art form is the creation of the slave culture that once existed in Brazil.

The practice of slavery is long gone, but *capoeira* still exists. In recent times, some social workers in Brazil have started using this unusual sport to help in educational and social development. This practice has become especially popular—and successful—with children and teenagers. An organization called 'Project **Axe**'[1] is leading the way in showing how *capoeira* can help young people.

---

[1] **Axe:** [aʃeɪ]

CD 3, Track 01

Skim for Gist

Read through the entire book quickly to answer the questions.

1. What is the reader basically about?
2. What is the role of *capoeira* in helping the street kids?

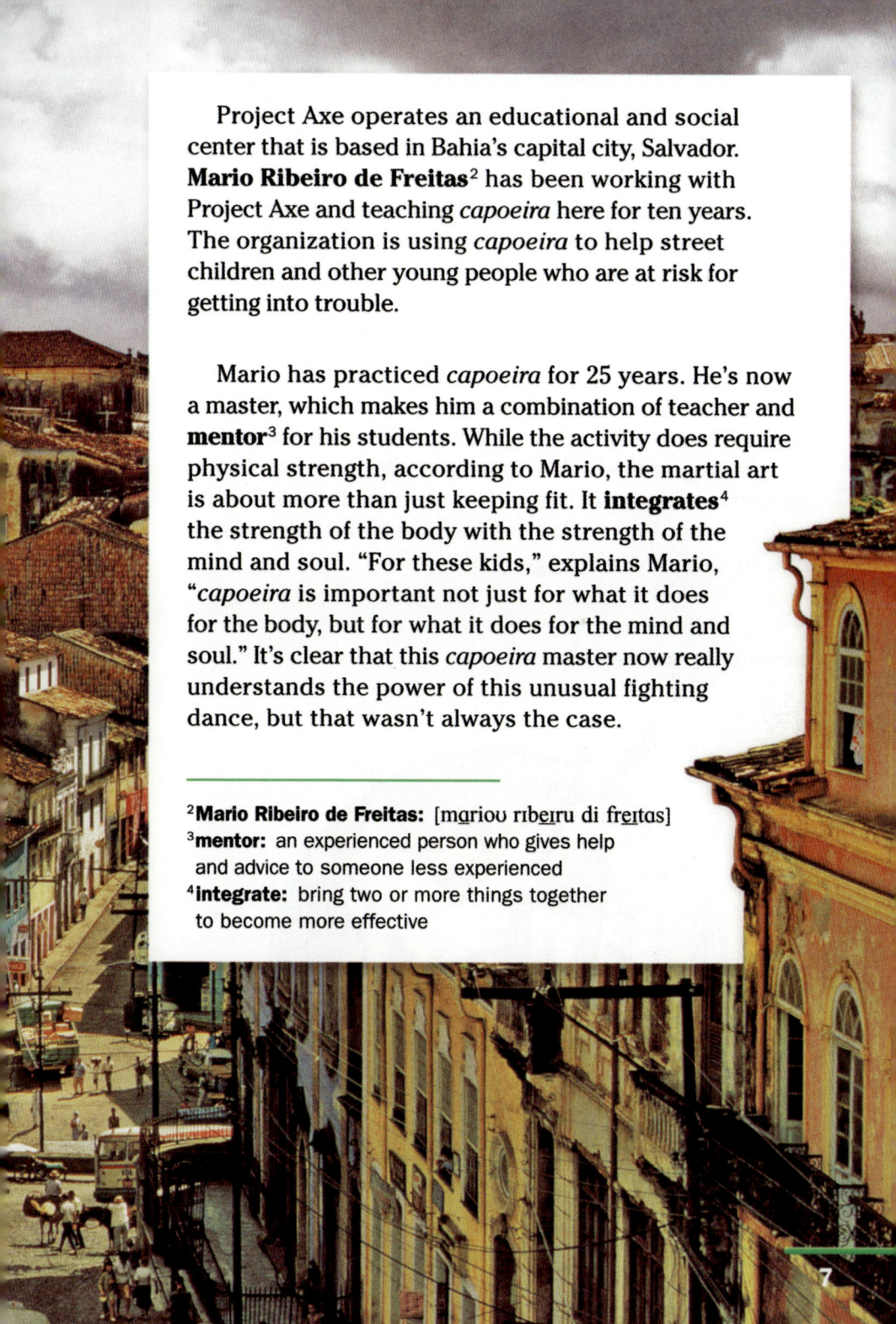

Project Axe operates an educational and social center that is based in Bahia's capital city, Salvador. **Mario Ribeiro de Freitas**[2] has been working with Project Axe and teaching *capoeira* here for ten years. The organization is using *capoeira* to help street children and other young people who are at risk for getting into trouble.

Mario has practiced *capoeira* for 25 years. He's now a master, which makes him a combination of teacher and **mentor**[3] for his students. While the activity does require physical strength, according to Mario, the martial art is about more than just keeping fit. It **integrates**[4] the strength of the body with the strength of the mind and soul. "For these kids," explains Mario, "*capoeira* is important not just for what it does for the body, but for what it does for the mind and soul." It's clear that this *capoeira* master now really understands the power of this unusual fighting dance, but that wasn't always the case.

---

[2] **Mario Ribeiro de Freitas:** [mɑriou rɪbeɪru di freɪtɑs]
[3] **mentor:** an experienced person who gives help and advice to someone less experienced
[4] **integrate:** bring two or more things together to become more effective

Years ago, Mario was just another young boy from a bad neighborhood, but then *capoeira* helped him, he says. "I studied with several *capoeira* masters and learned a **tremendous**[5] amount from them," he explains. "I took positive aspects from their lives and applied them to mine—not just to my teaching, but to my whole life, to my family," he adds.

Project Axe's programs are helping many of Salvador's children and teenagers who have run away from their homes. The participants may be in trouble with the police or be in programs which help people with drug problems. Axe workers make contact with many homeless kids out on the streets. Project Axe can help them, but first they have to make some changes.

---

[5]**tremendous:** very big; large

Young people who are interested in joining one of Axe's several educational programs must first agree to return to their own home or to go to a **foster home**.[6] Then, at the center, students can focus on music, dance, or fashion design in addition to *capoeira*. They can also receive help with their basic education.

Another important aspect of the program is that Project Axe works to make sure that the government knows about these kids. There are considerable numbers of street kids in parts of Brazil, some of whom have 'disappeared' from official records. Confirming that they have governmental records is very important for the futures of these young people. If they don't have any records, they often can't get jobs or even go to school. In this way, Project Axe is also an essential part of helping these kids to really belong and function in society.

---

[6]**foster home:** a home in a social system that receives money for taking care of children that cannot live in their own home

Fact Check: True or false?

1. Some of the young people in Project Axe have been in trouble with the police.

2. Mario didn't study *capoeira* until he was an adult.

3. Project Axe only helps kids who are no longer on the street.

4. Participants in the program can also study music.

Mario says that *capoeira* also teaches the students to control their behavior and to treat others with respect. He says that this is most apparent when participants form a circle and perform *capoeira* as a group, which is also known as 'the circle.' He explains in his own words: "Basically, I take what they have to offer—their body strength and their energy—and **mold**[7] it by integrating them into the group." He then talks about how he does this, "Once they are in the circle, which is the most **sacred**[8] moment of the *capoeira* process, I show them that there are **norms**,[9] rules, and limits—within yourself and with others—that need to be followed."

---

[7]**mold:** form into a shape
[8]**sacred:** held in high respect for religious or other reasons
[9]**norm:** rule; standard way of behaving

Capoeira has a long and interesting history. Hundreds of years ago, slaves in Brazil first practiced it as a way of opposing their owners. However, they made the fighting actions look like a dance so that their owners would not know what they were doing.

After slavery was **abolished**[10] in Brazil in 1888, *capoeira* became popular as both amusement and sport. It also helped to raise the ex-slaves' awareness of themselves as Afro-Brazilians, or Brazilians with African **heritage**.[11]

---

[10]**abolish:** stop; make illegal
[11]**heritage:** beliefs, traditions, history, etc. passed from parents to their children

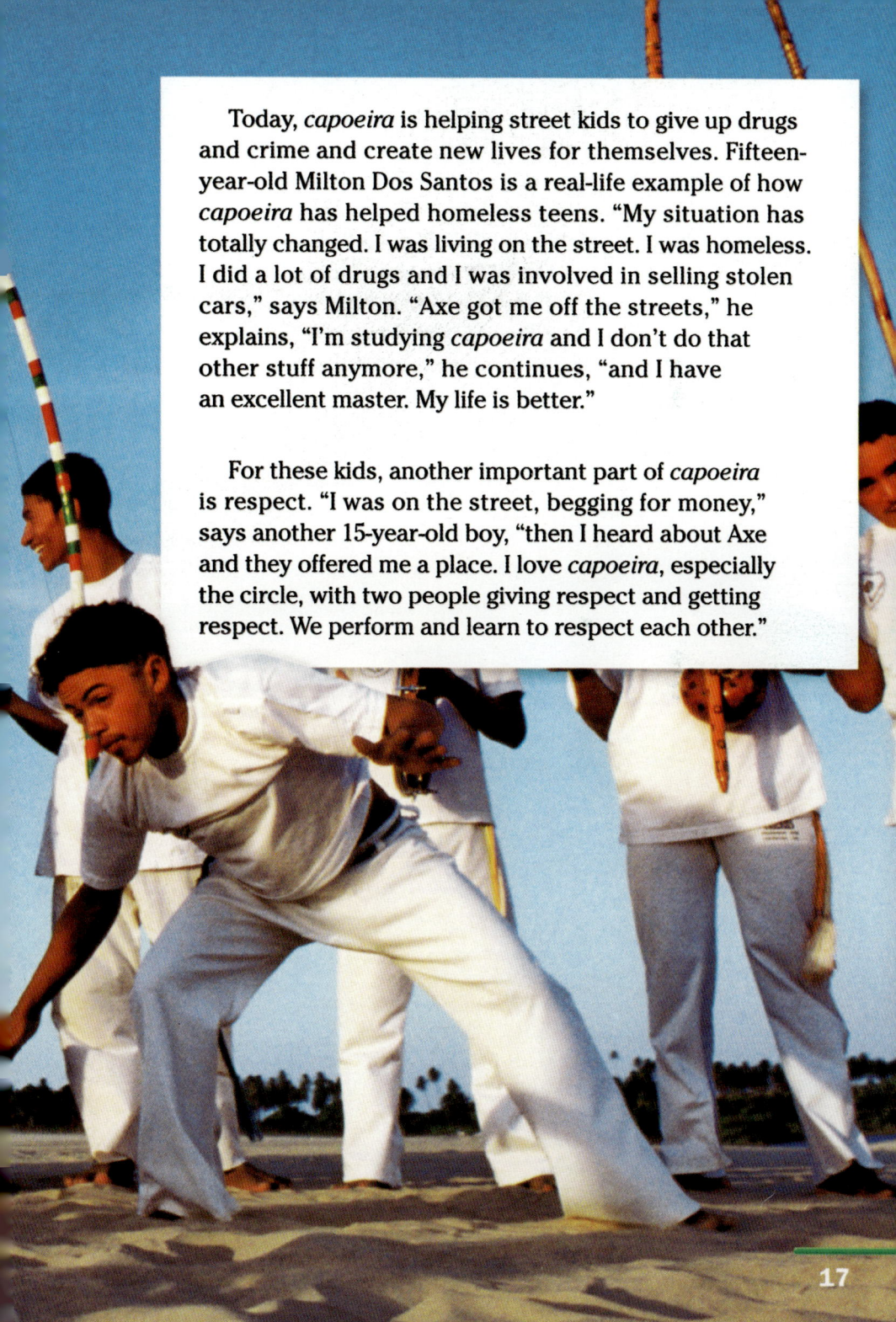

Today, *capoeira* is helping street kids to give up drugs and crime and create new lives for themselves. Fifteen-year-old Milton Dos Santos is a real-life example of how *capoeira* has helped homeless teens. "My situation has totally changed. I was living on the street. I was homeless. I did a lot of drugs and I was involved in selling stolen cars," says Milton. "Axe got me off the streets," he explains, "I'm studying *capoeira* and I don't do that other stuff anymore," he continues, "and I have an excellent master. My life is better."

For these kids, another important part of *capoeira* is respect. "I was on the street, begging for money," says another 15-year-old boy, "then I heard about Axe and they offered me a place. I love *capoeira*, especially the circle, with two people giving respect and getting respect. We perform and learn to respect each other."

In Mario's classroom at Project Axe, his students may still be a little nervous and a little unsure about their future, but there are signs of progress in their lives. One of his *capoeira* classes is now preparing for a two-week trip to Italy. They're going to perform for audiences there. It will be a long journey, but these young people have already come a long way. They've made it from the streets of Salvador to a safer, healthier place. The martial art of *capoeira* has given these young people hope for a better future.

After You Read

1. Who created *capoeira*?
   A. street kids
   B. social workers
   C. Brazilians in Africa
   D. slaves

2. Mario Riberio de Freitas has worked _____ Project Axe _____ years.
   A. on, in
   B. with, for
   C. for, during
   D. at, of

3. What does Mario think is the most important benefit of *capoeira*?
   A. strengthening the mind and soul
   B. learning protection
   C. developing physical power
   D. building a strong body

4. In paragraph 1 on page 8, in the phrase 'applied them,' to whom or what does 'them' refer?
   A. *capoeira* masters
   B. his family
   C. *capoeira* steps
   D. positive aspects

5. Children and teens who want to participate in Project Axe must first:
   A. go to Salvador
   B. talk to Mario
   C. stop being homeless
   D. create a foster home

6. The word 'basic' on page 10 can be replaced by:
   A. introductory
   B. new
   C. planned
   D. difficult

7. Brazilians need government records to:
   A. get a legal job
   B. find a foster home
   C. have children
   D. participate in Project Axe

8. Why does the writer give details about the *capoeira* circle?
   A. to show that *capoeira* is a religion
   B. to show who is the master
   C. to show that *capoeira* teaches social behavior
   D. to explain the rules that must be followed

9. Which of the following is a suitable heading for paragraph 1 page 14?
   A. A Modern Dance
   B. Secret Protection
   C. For Fun Only
   D. Dancing to Feel Free

10. What's the meaning of the word 'awareness' in paragraph 2 on page 14?
    A. society
    B. identity
    C. happiness
    D. knowledge

11. What's the main purpose of the views expressed on page 17?
    A. to describe lives improved by *capoeira*
    B. to explain why young people love to perform *capoeira*
    C. to show that street kids have a hard life
    D. to teach us about crime in Salvador

12. The young people in Project Axe have come a long way _____ a better life.
    A. on
    B. by
    C. in
    D. towards

 www.sport*blog.sa

CAPOEIRA CLUB
Capoeira Q and A

HOW CAN I FIND A CAPOEIRA SCHOOL?
POSTED: Peter on Sat Aug 9 @ 2:00 pm: I have checked several martial arts websites and I can't find a *capoeira* school in my area.

RE: HOW CAN I FIND A CAPOEIRA SCHOOL?
POSTED: Lionel on Sat Aug 9 @ 9:13 pm: Go to the home page for this website. In the upper left corner you will find a place to search for schools by city, state, or country. If you still can't find anything in your area, don't worry! We get lists of several new schools every day.

I WANT TO IMPROVE
POSTED: Daniel on Mon Aug 4 @ 5:01 pm: I've been practicing *capoeira* for about six months. I have learned a tremendous amount, but I want to get even better. It seems to take a long time to learn everything. Does anybody have any ideas for how I can improve quickly?

Capoeira Class at My School

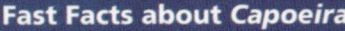

Fast Facts about *Capoeira*

- The countries with the most *capoeira* schools are Brazil (about 300) and the U.S. (over 500).

- In *capoeira*, a circle of people, called a *roda*, watch as two players compete in a fight-like dance called a *jugo*, or game.

- Music is an important part of *capoeira*. It sets the style and speed of the game.

- When a student is accepted into a *capoeira* group, he or she is given a belt (*corda*) and a special name (*apelido*).

RE: I WANT TO IMPROVE

POSTED: Marcia on Mon Aug 4 @ 7:44 pm: It takes time for your body to learn the movements and get strong. And it takes time for your mind to integrate what it needs to learn as well. However, here are some things that might help. Even though it may seem boring, find a mentor to help you practice the basics over and over again. Go to the gym and lift weights to help you get strong fast. You can also watch videos to learn new combinations of movements. Good luck!

WOMEN IN *CAPOEIRA*

POSTED: Maria on Mon Aug 4 @ 5:20 pm: I have discovered that if I hit a man while fighting, people think it's because he wasn't looking or he needs to improve his skills. But if I hit a woman, they think that it's just because she's a woman and they think I shouldn't have hit her. That really bothers me! Can't I treat men and women equally?

RE: WOMEN IN *CAPOEIRA*

POSTED: Ramon on Tue Aug 5 @ 1:00 am: Yes, you're right. It's not a fair way to look at things. A woman can kick and hit just as hard as a man, and they can avoid being hit just as well. Some women are better than men at *capoeira* and some men are better than women. We should assess the abilities of each person we fight individually.

CD 3, Track 02

Word Count: 388
Time: _____

Vocabulary List

abolish (14)
at risk (3, 7)
beg (3, 17)
combination (2, 4, 7)
crime (3, 17)
foster home (10)
heritage (14)
homeless (3, 8, 17)
integrate (7, 13)
martial art (2, 4, 7, 18)
master (2, 7, 8, 17)
mentor (7)
mold (13)
norm (13)
sacred (13)
slave (2, 4, 14)
social worker (3, 4)
soul (2, 7)
tremendous (8)